Two Strings To Your Bow by Robert Jephson

A FARCE, IN TWO ACTS. AS PERFORMED AT THE THEATRE-ROYAL, COVENT GARDEN.

Robert Jephson was born in Ireland in 1736, the son of Archdeacon John Jephson.

His education was at Ryder's grammar school and then the Reverend Roger Ford's school before he was admitted to Trinity College, Dublin in 1751. He left without a degree.

Jephson now joined the British Army with a commission in the 73rd Regiment of Foot. Among his postings was one to the Caribbean. He left, for health reasons and retired with the rank of Captain.

An appointment was offered as master of the horse to the lord-lieutenant of Ireland. Whilst in this office he wrote and had published, in the Mercury newspaper, a collection of articles that defended the lord-lieutenant's administration. These were later published in book form as 'The Bachelor', or 'Speculations of Jeoffry Wagstaffe'.

Jepson held the office under twelve successive viceroys and gained a pension of £300, which was later doubled.

He entered the Irish House of Commons in 1773 and sat for St Johnstown (County Longford) until 1776. Between 1777 and 1783, he served as Member of Parliament for Old Leighlin and thereafter represented Granard from 1783 to 1790

In 1775 he added playwright, dramatist and poet to his military and political career strands. His plays gathered much interest. Among them his tragedy 'Braganza' was successfully performed at Drury Lane in 1775, 'Conspiracy' in 1796, 'The Law of Lombardy' in 1779, and 'The Count of Narbonne' (adapted from Horace Walpole's 'The Castle of Otranto') at Covent Garden in 1781.

In 1788 he published 'Extempore Ludicrous Miltonic Verses' and, in 1794, the heroic poem 'Roman Portraits', and 'The Confessions of Jacques Baptiste Couteau', a satire on the excesses of the French Revolution.

Robert Jephson died at Blackrock, near Dublin, on the 31st of May 1803.

Index of Contents

I0158436

Don Pedro,	Mr Waddy.
Don Sancho,	Mr Atkins.
Octavio,	Mr Farley.
Ferdinand,	Mr Claremont.
Borachio,	Mr Davenport.
Lazarillo,	Mr Munden.
Porter,	Mr Platt.
1st Waiter,	Mr Abbot.
2nd Waiter,	Mr Truman.
Donna Clara,	Mrs St Leger.
Leonora,	Miss Searle.
Maid,	Miss Leserpe.

TWO STRINGS TO YOUR BOW

ACT I

SCENE I.—Don Pedro's House

Enter **DON SANCHO**, **DON PEDRO**, and **BORACHIO**.

DON SANCHO
Here's my hand. Is it a bargain?

DON PEDRO
Certainly—we'll have the wedding to-night. The young couple are so much in love, they will be glad to dispense with ceremony—it really looks as if heaven had a hand in this match, for if young Felix had not died so commodiously at Salamanca, we could never have been brothers-in-law.

BORACHIO
Bless me, your honour! is poor Don Felix dead then? he was a merry young gentleman—I'm sorry for it with all my soul.

DON PEDRO
Ay, he is as dead as King Philip the Second—but did you know Don Felix?

BORACHIO
As well as any hogshead in my cellar—I have kept a tavern three years at Salamanca, and he was my constant customer. I knew his sister too, a brave mettled damsel, that made no more of clapping on a pair of breeches, and straddling a horse-back, than if she had never been laced in stays, or encumbered with a petticoat.

DON PEDRO

Well, now she may give a more free scope to her frolics, for she has no brother left to restrain her. We sent for you, Borachio, to provide the wedding dinner. Let things be as they should be.

BORACHIO

Never trouble your head about it. I'll set you out such a repast—the first course shall be as substantial as the bridegroom, and the second as delicate as the bride—then for wines and a dessert! I don't care if you ask all the Benedictines to sit in judgment upon their flavour and freshness.

[Enter a **SERVANT MAID**.

MAID

Sir, there's a servant of a strange gentleman, who has a message for you.

DON PEDRO

What does he want with me?

MAID

He will not tell his business to any one but your worship. He has been fooling with me till I am tired with him.

DON PEDRO

Bid him come in.

[Exit **MAID**.

DON SANCHO

Can you guess what business a stranger can have with you?

DON PEDRO

Ay, I suppose the old business—some needy spendthrift, who has lost his purse at the gaming-table, and wants to try if I am fool enough to take a liking to him, and lend him as much more upon his no security.

[Enter **LAZARILLO** and **MAID**.

LAZARILLO

I have the honour to be, gentlemen, with the most profound respect, your honour's most faithful, obsequious, and obedient humble servant.

DON SANCHO

This fellow begins his speech like the conclusion of a letter.

DON PEDRO

Have you any business with me, friend?

LAZARILLO

May I take the liberty to ask your honour a question?

DON PEDRO
Ay, what is it?

LAZARILLO
Pray, who may that pretty, plump, cherry-cheeked, round-hipped, buxom, genteel, light-pastern'd, black-eyed damsel be?

DON PEDRO
What business is it of your's? she's my daughter's maid.

LAZARILLO
I wish your honour much joy of her.

DON PEDRO
What does the fellow mean? to your business, friend—who are you? what do you want with me? who do you belong to?

LAZARILLO
Softly, softly, sir: three questions in a breath are too much for a poor man like me to answer all at once.

DON PEDRO [To **DON SANCHO**]
I don't know what to make of this fellow—I believe he is none of the wisest.

DON SANCHO
I should rather suspect he was none of the honestest.

LAZARILLO
Are you married, my pretty lass?

DON PEDRO
What would the fellow be at? what's your business, I say?

LAZARILLO
Sir, to answer your questions—in the first place, I am my master's servant.
[To the **MAID**]
And my pretty one, as I was going to tell you, if the Don had not interrupted me—

DON PEDRO
Who the devil is your master?

LAZARILLO
He's a strange gentleman, sir, who has a strong inclination to pay your worship a visit.
[To the **MAID**]
And now as to the little affair between us—

DON PEDRO
Who is this strange gentleman? what business has he with me?

LAZARILLO
Sir, he is the noble Don Felix de Silva, of Salamanca, who waits below to have the supreme felicity of kissing your honour's hand, and has sent me before to make his compliments to you.
[To the **MAID**]
Well, my dear, have you thought of the proposal? do you think me shocking?

DON PEDRO
Mind me, fellow—what is this you say?

LAZARILLO
Sir, if you are curious to know particulars about me, I am Lazarillo, of Valencia, as honest a little fellow, though I say it, that should not say it, as ever rode before a portmanteau.
[To the **MAID**]
What I pride myself for, more than any other good quality, is, that I am the adorer, and faithful slave of your divine and insurmountable beauty.

DON PEDRO
Turn this way, booby—you are either drunk or mad—why, Don Felix, of Salamanca, is dead.

[Exit **MAID**.

LAZARILLO
Dead!

DON SANCHO
You may get another master, honest friend, for poor Don Felix has no occasion for you.

LAZARILLO
This is strange news. It must be a very sudden death—perhaps it was only his ghost that hired me, but I never saw any thing so like a living creature; he gave me a rap over the shoulders just now, that I thought felt very natural. If he is really a ghost, he won't dare to pretend he's alive, and tell a lie before so much good company.

[Exit.

DON PEDRO
What do you think of this rascal? Is he a knave, or a fool?

BORACHIO
To my thinking, he's a brewing of both.

DON SANCHO
To my poor thinking, he's crazy.

DON PEDRO
'Fore heaven, brother-in-law that is to be, if Don Felix should be alive, we two should make but a silly figure.

[Re-enter **LAZARILLO**.

LAZARILLO
Truly, gentlemen, this is but indifferent treatment for a stranger, to tell a poor servant like me that his master was dead.

DON PEDRO
So he is. I say.

LAZARILLO
And I say that he is not only alive, but in good health, sound as a biscuit, and sprightly as champaigne—and at this moment is ready to come in, and give you proof positive by your own eye-sight.

DON SANCHO
What, Don Felix?

LAZARILLO
Ay, Don Felix.

DON PEDRO
De Silva?

LAZARILLO
Ay, De Silva.

DON SANCHO
Of Salamanca?

LAZARILLO
Ay, of Salamanca.

DON PEDRO
I would recommend to you, friend, to lose a little blood, and have your head shaved—you are mad.

LAZARILLO
This is enough to make me so: I say he is below at this moment waiting in the parlour.

DON PEDRO
I'll break your head, you rascal.

DON SANCHO
Keep your temper. Stay, let us see this impostor, who calls himself Don Felix. Bid him walk up stairs.

DON PEDRO
Ay, ay, you're right—let's see this resurrection.

LAZARILLO

In a twinkling.

[Exit **LAZARILLO**.

DON SANCHO
This is some sham, some cheat; but I think we sha'n't be easily imposed upon.

DON PEDRO
Let me alone, let me alone, he must rise early, brother, who makes a fool of Don Pedro.

[Enter **DONNA CLARA**, in Men's Clothes.

DONNA CLARA
Signior Don Pedro, after the many polite letters I have received from you, I could little expect such extraordinary treatment, to be kept half an hour cooling my heels among muleteers and lacquies.

DON PEDRO
Sir, I humbly ask your pardon. But may I take the liberty to crave your name, or title?

DONNA CLARA
My name, sir, is Don Felix de Silva.

DON PEDRO
Of Salamanca?

DONNA CLARA
The same.

BORACHIO [Aside]
Ha, what's this? why this is Donna Clara, the sister of Felix: let's see what will be the end of this.

DON PEDRO
I'm struck dumb with amazement; sir, I rejoice to see you safe and sound, which, indeed, is a little extraordinary, considering we had heard you was dead and buried.
[Aside to **DON SANCHO**]
I wish, with all my heart, he was under ground.

DONNA CLARA
It was reported, I know, that I was dead; but in fact, I only received a flesh wound in a quarrel; a fainting fit succeeded the loss of blood, and gave occasion to the report of my death: but the moment I recovered strength enough to travel, I mounted my horse, and set out to pay my respects, and keep my engagement.

DON PEDRO
I really don't know what to say to it: you have the appearance of a gentleman; but I have had such assurances that Don Felix was dead, that, unless I have some strong proofs to the contrary—you'll pardon me, sir,—I mean no harm—but, truly, in a matter of this consequence, a little caution, you know—

DONNA CLARA
Sir, you're perfectly right; but here are proofs—here are no less than four letters. This is from the governor of the Bank—you know the hand and seal, I suppose.

BORACHIO [To **DONNA CLARA**]
Sir, will you permit me to congratulate you upon your recovery, and your arrival in Granada?

DONNA CLARA [Aside]
Ha! confusion! my old host of Salamanca—he'll certainly know and will discover me. I think I recollect you, friend.

BORACHIO
I believe you may, your honour; my face is no stranger at Salamanca; Joseph Borachio is as well known as the high road to Madrid.

DONNA CLARA [Aside to **BORACHIO**]
True, true, I knew I was acquainted with you—hark! a word—don't betray me, and this purse has a twin brother as like it—

BORACHIO
Never fear, madam: there's something so engaging in your countenance, and so persuasive in your manner, that I would as soon pull down my sign as discover you.
[Aside to **DONNA CLARA**]
Aloud. I am, for want of a better, the master of the Eagle, hard by: and will be bold to say, that, for good treatment, soft beds, wholesome food, and old wine, Joseph Borachio will not give the wall to any publican in Granada.

DONNA CLARA
Get your best apartments ready, and I'll order my baggage there.

DON PEDRO
Why, certainly these letters are addressed to Don Felix; but there are ways, you know, of getting another man's letters—at the same time, sir—

DONNA CLARA
Nay, sir, if you still doubt, here's my old acquaintance, Joseph Borachio, he knows me; I suppose you'll take his word, though you seem a little suspicious of mine.

BORACHIO
Lord, sir, I'll give my oath to him.
[Aside]
I'll tell twenty lies every bill I bring up for half a dollar, and the devil's in my conscience if I can't tell one for a purse of doubloons.

[Exit.

DON PEDRO

Sir, I ask a thousand pardons: my doubts are vanished; you certainly are Don Felix.
[To **DON SANCHO**]
What do you think of this, brother-in-law that was to be?

DON SANCHO
Why I think it is a little unlucky, that the dead should get out of their graves to prevent our being relations.

[Enter **FERDINAND** and **LEONORA**.

LEONORA
Did you send for me, father?

DON PEDRO
I did send for you, my dear; but matters are a little changed within this half-hour.

DONNA CLARA
Is that young lady your daughter, Don Pedro?

DON PEDRO
Ay, sir, that is my daughter.

DONNA CLARA
This then is the young lady I must pay my addresses to—I hope, madam, the consent of our families to my happiness, has made no unfavourable impression against the person of your humble servant.

LEONORA
What can I say to him—yes, sir—no, sir—

DONNA CLARA
An odd reception!—yes, sir—no, sir—pray, sir,—
[To **DON PEDRO**]
—how am I to understand the lady?

DON PEDRO
She's a little bashful at present—she'll be more intelligible by and by—she is not much acquainted with you yet—she'll come to presently.

DONNA CLARA
I hope so—this gentleman—
[To **FERDINAND**]
I suppose, is a friend of the family—a near relation.

FERDINAND
A friend of the family certainly; but no other way a relation, than as I am to call this lady my wife.

DON SANCHO [Aside]

Right! stick to that—don't give up your pretensions—my boy has spirit—that young coxcomb won't carry it so swimmingly.

DONNA CLARA
How's this? I don't understand you, sir,—your wife?—what, does that lady intend to have two husbands?

DON PEDRO
Young gentleman, pray come with me; here has been a small mistake. Your supposed death—but I'll explain every thing to you within—depend upon it I shall fulfil my engagements.

FERDINAND
But hark'ee, sir, I suppose you are a cavalier of honour, and don't imagine that the affections of a young lady are thrown into the bargain when the old folks are pleased to strike up a contract—you'll ask Donna Leonora's consent, I hope.

DONNA CLARA
I don't know that. People of fashion never embarrass themselves with such vulgar ideas. Lawyers do all that's necessary on such occasions; if the conveyances are right, affection and that old stuff, follow of course, you know.

DON SANCHO
I suppose he'd marry a mermaid if there was a good fishing bank entailed upon her.

DONNA CLARA
Sir, I have not been so unsuccessful in gallantry, as to apprehend that the lady will object to me.

FERDINAND
Sir, I perceive you have a very favourable opinion of yourself; but it would be more to the purpose if you could persuade the lady to have the same partiality. But, sir, a word in your ear. You and I must talk of this matter in another place; you understand me.

[Touches his Sword, and exit.

DON SANCHO
Bravo! well said—he's a chip of the old block—Don Pedro, or brother-in-law that was to be, you and I must talk of this matter in another place—you understand me.

[Touches his Sword, and exit.

DON PEDRO
Oh Lord! oh Lord!

DONNA CLARA
But, charming Leonora, these gallants are so warm, they have not allowed you an opportunity to speak for yourself. What do you say to me, fair creature?

LEONORA

I say that I look at you with horror, and that my evil genius sent you here to destroy my happiness.

[Exit.

DON PEDRO
What will become of me! I shall have a quarrel with that old ruffian in spite of me. I'll after him, and try what can be done with my daughter by coaxing: if that fails, I must even have recourse to the old fatherly expedients of locking up, and a diet of bread and water.

DONNA CLARA
Hold a moment—for heaven's sake no harshness. Leave your daughter to me a little time, and my attention may, perhaps, bring her to reason. But in the interim, sir, as I have occasion for some ready cash, and my letters of credit are upon you, I must trouble you for two hundred pistoles.

DON PEDRO
With pleasure, sir. I have not so much cash about me, but if you will take the trouble just to step into the next street—

DONNA CLARA
I am much obliged to you, and will take the liberty to send my servant. I can depend upon his honesty.

[Exeunt.

SCENE II.—Changes to the Hotel

Enter **BORACHIO**.

BORACHIO
Well, I know not how this will end for other folks, but it has had a very promising beginning for me already—a hundred pistoles for keeping a secret, which I could not get a maravedi for discovering. Then there can be no fault found with my charges or my entertainment, though I serve up crows for partridges, and a delicate ram-cat for a fricasee of rabbits. But here comes my adventurer.

[Enter to him **DONNA CLARA**.

DONNA CLARA
Borachio! a word with you! As you know who I am, 'tis to no purpose to make a secret of any part of my history: my brother, you know, is dead, died at Salamanca; but you don't yet understand why I have assumed his sex and character.

BORACHIO
I shall be glad to learn it, my sweet young lady; especially if I can be of any service to you.

DONNA CLARA
My poor brother made too free with some choice wine at a vento near Salamanca. Octavio, my lover, happened to be of the party; a quarrel ensued between my brother's company and a set of strangers,

who had just arrived at the same place; in the fray my brother was run through the body, and left dead on the spot; the officers of justice had orders to search for, and seize all who were present as principals in the murder; to avoid the pursuit, Octavio, as I was informed, fled hither; and with the wardrobe, credentials, and the name of my brother, here I have followed him.

BORACHIO
Ay, madam, you was always a young lady of spirit, and 'egad! I love spirit: and though I was never to touch a pistole of the other purse you was pleased to promise me, I would no more tell your secret than I would tell my guests my own secret, how I turn Alicant into Burgundy, and sour cyder into Champagne of the first growth of France.

DONNA CLARA
I rely upon you. But I wish to see my apartment; pray enquire for my servant, and bid him come to me immediately. I ordered him to wait for me near the Prado.

BORACHIO
May I ask where you picked up that fellow?

DONNA CLARA
I found him on my journey. He's an odd mixture of simplicity and cunning; but I have no reason to suspect his honesty, and that's the quality for which at present I have most occasion.

[Exeunt.

SCENE III.—A Hall in the Hotel

LAZARILLO alone.

LAZARILLO
My master desired me to wait for him in the street, but I see no sign of him—'tis twelve by the clock, but by my guts at least four. There is no watch, clock, or pendulum in the city, that points to the dining hour with more certainty than the mechanism of my bowels: I feel a craving that must be satisfied. Odzooks! what a delicate flavour of roast, boiled, and baked, issues from these purlieus! the very smell is enough to create an appetite. Ay, that way lies the kitchen—I know it by the attraction of the odour. I'll down— but hold, not a sous, by Fortune; my purse is as empty as my belly.

[Enter **OCTAVIO**, a drunken **PORTER** following with a Portmanteau.

OCTAVIO
Come along, you drunken rascal!

PORTER
Not a step further without payment.

OCTAVIO
Why, scoundrel! would you have your hire before you earn it?

PORTER
Ay, that I would—as I'd like to make sure of my straw before I was to sleep on it—pay me directly, or here I stick as fast as a mule up to the girths in the mire.

OCTAVIO
Carry in the portmanteau—there's the door, carry in the portmanteau—'tis not three yards, you sot you.

PORTER
Sot in your teeth—pay me.

[Throws down the portmanteau.

LAZARILLO
What's this! egad, I may get something by it—it has an omen of dinner—I smell beef in it.

[Goes up to the **PORTER**.

Why, you drunken, staggering sputtering beast of burden, with two legs and no conscience, how dare you prate so saucily to a gentleman? reel off, or I'll teach you manners.

[Beats off the **PORTER**, and then carries in the portmanteau.

OCTAVIO
A good smart fellow—that looks like a servant; if he has no master, I'll hire him.

[Re-enter **LAZARILLO**.

Come hither, friend—do you know me?

LAZARILLO
No, sir, I only know that you are a gentleman—that is, I don't know you are a gentleman, but I have a strong suspicion of it. You look for all the world as if you would not let a man who wanted his dinner, and had an excellent stomach, go without it.

OCTAVIO
Are you acquainted with the tavern?

LAZARILLO
I think I am very well acquainted with it. The cellars are full of old wine, the larder full of butcher's meat and poultry—'twould make a man's mouth water but to look at them. Sir, does your honour smell nothing?

OCTAVIO
Smell!—no.

LAZARILLO

Lord bless me, sir! why, there are such steams from savoury pies, such a fumette from plump partridges, and roasting pigs, that I think I can distinguish them as easily as I know a rose from a pink, or jonquil from a cauliflower.

OCTAVIO
Are you at present in service? have you any master?

LAZARILLO [Aside]
I'll tell a bouncing lie, and disown my master.—No, sir.

OCTAVIO
You seem to be a ready intelligent fellow—will you be my servant?

LAZARILLO
Will I eat when I'm hungry? will I sleep when I'm weary? can your honour doubt it? command me, sir, from one extremity of the kingdom to the other; give me but as much as will keep cold air out of my stomach, and I can never tire in your service. Then, as for wages, to be sure my last master was a very princely sort of a gentleman—he gave me, sir—

OCTAVIO
No matter what—I sha'n't be more difficult to please, or less generous to reward, than he was. What's your name?

LAZARILLO
Lazarillo, sir.

OCTAVIO
I will employ you immediately. Go to the post-house—take this pistole—enquire if there are any letters for Don Octavio, of Salamanca, and bring them here to me.

[**OCTAVIO** goes in.

[**LAZARILLO** alone.

Well done, Lazarillo; between two stools they say a certain part of a man comes to the ground; but 'tis hard, indeed, if I don't take care of myself between two masters.

[Enter to him **DONNA CLARA** and **BORACHIO**.

DONNA CLARA
So, my gentleman, this is your attention to my commands? I ordered you to wait for me at the Prado: I might have looked for you, it seems, till morning, if by mere accident I had not found you here.

LAZARILLO
By your honour's leave, I waited for you till my very bowels began to yearn; such a craving came upon me, that had pikes, pistols, and petteraroes opposed my passage, I could not avoid entering the house in hopes of—

DONNA CLARA
No prating. Go directly, order my baggage to be brought hither, then run to the post, and enquire if there are any letters for Don Felix, or Donna Clara, of Salamanca, and bring them to me directly.

LAZARILLO
Here, sir?

DONNA CLARA
Yes, here to this hotel.

[Exit.

LAZARILLO [Aside]
Zounds! what shall I do with my other master?

BORACHIO
The post-office is but in the next street; if you should miss your way returning, enquire for me.

LAZARILLO
For you! and pray, who are you, sir?

BORACHIO
Joseph Borachio, the master of the Eagle: every body knows me.

LAZARILLO
So, sir, you are master of this house?

BORACHIO
I am.

LAZARILLO
Then you are a happy man. I had a respect for the roundness of your belly, and the illumination of your nose, the first glimpse I had of you; but now my respect is increased to adoration. If you leave money for masses for your soul, take my advice, get the fathers, instead of praying you out of purgatory into Paradise, to pray you back into your own kitchen. In my opinion, no Paradise can be superior to it.

[Exit.

[Enter **OCTAVIO**, at an opposite Door to **BORACHIO**.

OCTAVIO
If this be true that Felix is still alive, I need conceal myself no longer: you say you saw him?

BORACHIO
Saw him! yes, sir; saw him and conversed with him.

OCTAVIO

A very sudden recovery! but since 'tis so, I have no business here; I'll just send for my letters, and then back to Salamanca. Borachio!

BORACHIO
Sir!

OCTAVIO
Let me have horses ready, I shall set out this evening.

BORACHIO
This evening! why your honour has had no time to refresh yourself. Our roads of late are none of the safest after sun-set. Why, sir, not above a week ago, a calash of mine with a young cavalier and his new-married bride, were attacked on the road by six of the most desperate banditti that ever cried stand to a traveller.

OCTAVIO
Indeed!

BORACHIO
Too true, sir. Two of my best mules were shot dead at the first discharge of their carbines; they wounded the gentleman, stunned my drivers, and rifled the poor young lady in a terrible manner. In truth, your honour had better not think of venturing till morning, when you have the day fairly before you.

OCTAVIO
No, hang it! such fellows seldom attack a single traveller; besides, if your horses are good, I think I could out-gallop them.

BORACHIO
I'll answer for the horses, better never came out of Andalusia: they have straw up to their withers, and barley they may bury their ears in: poor dumb beasts, I take as much care of them, and love them as well, as if they were my fellow Christians.

OCTAVIO
What noise is that? away, landlord, and order the horses.

[Exit.

[Enter **LAZARILLO**, with **PORTERS** following him.

LAZARILLO
This way, this way, my lads—what the deuce, my last master's here still!
[To the **PORTERS**]
Fall back, rascals, and wait for me in the passage.

[Exeunt **PORTERS**.

OCTAVIO

Lazarillo!

LAZARILLO
Sir!

OCTAVIO
I shall set out for Salamanca presently.

LAZARILLO
Before dinner, sir?

OCTAVIO
Yes, directly.

LAZARILLO
Mercy on me! no pity on my stomach. Truly, sir, I am but a bad traveller on an empty belly; I get such whims and vertigoes, the wind plays such vagaries in the hollow crannies of my entrails, that you would have more trouble with me than if I were a sick baboon.

OCTAVIO
I sent you to the post; where are my letters? quick, quick—what are you fumbling about?

LAZARILLO
Patience, sir, a little patience. I thought I put them into this pocket—no, they are not there—then they must be in the other pocket.
[Aside]
The letters are so unwilling to come out for fear they should be obliged to bear witness against me; I have mixed the letters of both my masters, and curse me if I know which I ought to give him.

OCTAVIO
You tedious booby! where are my letters?

LAZARILLO
Here, sir, here are three of them; but they are not all for your honour. I'll tell you, sir, how I came by them. As I was going to the post, I met an old fellow-servant, who happened to be in a great hurry upon another errand, and he desired me to ask for his master's letters, and keep them for him. One of them belongs to him, but which I don't know, for to tell you the truth, sir, my parents found I had such fine natural parts, they would not throw away money in having me taught any thing, so reading was left out among some other accomplishments in my education.

OCTAVIO
Let me see them. I'll take my own, and give you back what belongs to your friend's master.

[Takes the Letters.

What's this? to Donna Clara—in Granada!

LAZARILLO

Have you found the letter, sir, that belongs to my comrade?

OCTAVIO
Who is your comrade?

LAZARILLO
An old fellow servant of mine; a very honest fellow, I have known him from a boy, when he was not this high, please your honour.

OCTAVIO
His name, puppy?

LAZARILLO
His name, sir—his name—Lopez, sir—

OCTAVIO
Where does this Lopez live?

LAZARILLO
Starve me if I can tell, sir.

OCTAVIO
How then could you know where to carry him the letter?

LAZARILLO
Oh, for that matter, sir, I'll tell your honour that in a moment.

OCTAVIO
Well, out with it.

LAZARILLO [Putting his hand to his cheek]
Deuce take it! I am stung to the bone I believe.

OCTAVIO
What's the matter?

LAZARILLO
A muskito, sir, a little peevish, whizzing, blood sucking vermin!

OCTAVIO
Where, I say, were you to meet Lopez?

LAZARILLO
I ask pardon, sir—in the Piazza.

OCTAVIO
What am I to think of this?

LAZARILLO
Dear Fortune—get me out of this puzzle—
[Aside]
Won't your honour give me my comrade's letter?

OCTAVIO
No, I have occasion for it; I must open it.

LAZARILLO
Open another gentleman's letter! why, sir, 'tis reckoned one of the most unmannerly pieces of
friendship a gentleman can be guilty of.

OCTAVIO
Peace, I say—I am too much interested to mind forms at present.
[Reads]
"Madam,
"Your sudden departure from Salamanca has occasioned the greatest consternation among your friends.
They have made all possible enquiries, and have discovered that you left this town in your brother's
clothes, and the general opinion is, that you are gone in pursuit of Octavio, who was known to pay his
addresses to you at Salamanca. I shall not fail to communicate any further intelligence of your affairs
which comes to my knowledge, and I remain with great respect,
Manuel."

LAZARILLO [Aside]
He little cares what may happen to me from his curiosity.

OCTAVIO
Clara fled from Salamanca, and in pursuit of me! find this Lopez instantly, bring him here, and I'll reward
him for his intelligence.

LAZARILLO
Yes, sir, give me the letter that belongs to him. But how am I to account for its being opened? This may
bring an imputation upon my honour, about which I am amazingly punctilious.

OCTAVIO
Your honour, mongrel! say the letter was opened by mistake, and instantly find Lopez.

[Exit.

[**LAZARILLO** alone.

LAZARILLO
Find Lopez! 'gad if I do I shall be a lucky fellow, for I know no such person. Lazarillo, thou hast a head-
piece never fails thee at a pinch: if I could but read and write, I'd turn author, and invent tales and story-
books. But what the deuce shall I say about opening the letter? let me see! is there no way to disguise
it? I remember my mother used to make wafers with bread and water. I have a few crumbs in my
pocket, and with a little mouth-moistening—I don't see why it should not answer; here goes for an
experiment.

[Takes bread out of his Pocket, and chews it.

Gadzooks! it has slipped down my throat—it would not go against nature. My mouth's like the hole of a till, whatever goes in falls to the bottom. I'll take more care this time. There it is—

[Seals the Letter.

I think it will do. After all, what signifies how a letter's sealed, provided he likes the contents of it.

[Enter **DONNA CLARA**.

DONNA CLARA
Was you at the post? did you get my letter?

LAZARILLO
Yes, sir, there it is.

[Gives the Letter.

DONNA CLARA
Why this letter has been opened.

LAZARILLO
Impossible.

DONNA CLARA
I say it has, and here it has been patched up again with a piece of bread.

LAZARILLO
Egad, that's very extraordinary.

DONNA CLARA [Seizing him]
Confess, villain, what trick has been played with my letter—the truth instantly, or—

LAZARILLO
Hold, sir, have a little patience, and I'll tell the truth: if you frighten me, I shall never be able to tell it.

DONNA CLARA
Quick then, this moment.

LAZARILLO
Then, sir, it was I opened it.

DONNA CLARA
Impudent varlet! for what purpose?

LAZARILLO

A mistake, nothing but a mistake, as I am a Christian: I thought it was directed to me, and I opened it.

DONNA CLARA
And read it?

LAZARILLO
No, sir, no, upon my veracity, I read nothing but the first word, and finding it was not for me, I clapped in a wafer directly just as your honour sees it.

DONNA CLARA
You are sure no other person saw it?

LAZARILLO
Sure of it! I'll take my oath. As I am an honest man, as I hope to die in my bed—if your honour has a book about you, I'll swear by it. Any other person! no, no,—lord, sir, I never was so much grieved in my life as when it was opened, I gave myself a great knock in the head for vexation. I believe you may see the mark of it here just over my left eye-brow.

[**DONNA CLARA** reads the Letter.

LAZARILLO
There's something in that letter does not please him. I shall have enough to do to manage my two masters.

DONNA CLARA
There are the keys of my baggage, get my things ready for dressing.

[Exit.

[Enter **DON PEDRO**, at an opposite Door.

DON PEDRO
Is your master at home?

LAZARILLO
No, sir.

DON PEDRO
Do you expect him back to dinner?

LAZARILLO
O yes, by all means, sir.

DON PEDRO
Give him this purse when he returns, with my compliments—there are two hundred pistoles in it.—I shall wait upon him myself in the evening.

[Gives a Purse to **LAZARILLO**, and exit.

LAZARILLO
Yes, sir—but curse me if I know which of my masters 'tis intended for. I'll offer it to the first of them I see, and if it does not belong to him, I suppose he won't take it.

[Enter **OCTAVIO**.

OCTAVIO
Have you found Lopez?

LAZARILLO
No, sir, not yet, but I have found a better thing for you.

OCTAVIO
A better thing! what's that?

LAZARILLO
Only a purse—full of money. I believe there are two hundred pistoles in it.

OCTAVIO
I suppose it was left by my banker.

LAZARILLO
You expected money, sir?

OCTAVIO
Yes, I left a letter of credit with him.

LAZARILLO
Oh, then there can be no doubt it was left for you, sir. Give it to your master, says he—yes, sir, says I; so there's the money.

OCTAVIO
Hold! lock up this money till I want it—take care—put it up safely, for I shall soon have occasion for it. But go find Lopez, and bring him to me immediately.

[Exit.

LAZARILLO [Alone]
Go find Lopez, and bring him to me immediately—but where I shall find him, is another matter—I'll go look for what I am sure of finding, a good dinner. What a fortunate fellow was I not to make any mistake about the money!—if a man takes care in great matters, small matters will take care of themselves—or if they should go wrong, if the gusts of ill-luck should make his vessel drive a little, honesty is a sheet-anchor, and always brings him up to his birth again.

[Exit.

Enter **DONNA CLARA** and **LEONORA**.

DONNA CLARA
I have told you my story; I rely upon your honour, you will not discover me.

LEONORA
Don't fear me. You have relieved me from such anxiety by your friendly confidence, that I would rather die than betray you; nay, what is still more, I would rather lose my lover.

DONNA CLARA
Of that there can be no danger; let matters proceed to the utmost, the discovery of my sex puts an end, at once, to any impediment from my claim to you.

LEONORA
But may I not tell Ferdinand?

DONNA CLARA
No. Pray indulge me; a secret burns in a single breast; it is just possible that two may keep it, but if 'tis known to a third, I might as well tell it to the crier, and have it proclaimed at the great door of every church in Granada.

LEONORA
Well, you shall be obeyed; depend upon it I will be faithful to you. Men give themselves strange airs about our sex: we are so unaccustomed, they say, to be trusted, that our vanity of a confidence shews we are unworthy of it.

DONNA CLARA
No matter what they say: I think half of their superiority lies in their beards and their doublets.

DON PEDRO [Within]
Leonora!

LEONORA
My father calls me; farewell, dear Clara! should you want my assistance, you know you may command me.

[Exit.

[Enter **FERDINAND**.

FERDINAND
So, sir, I have found you. Do you know me, sir?

DONNA CLARA
I have so many acquaintance whom I should wish not to know, that I don't like to answer that question suddenly.

FERDINAND
Do you take me for a sharper, youngster?

DONNA CLARA
Sharpers wear good clothes.

FERDINAND
And puppies wear long swords.—What means that piece of steel dangling there by thy effeminate side? Is thy soft hand too weak to touch it? Death! to be rivalled by a puppet, by a thing made of cream! Why, thou compound of fringe, lace, and powder, darest thou pretend to win a lady's affections? answer, stripling, can'st thou fight for a lady?

DONNA CLARA [Aside]
He's a terrible fellow! I quake every inch of me; but I must put a good face upon it—I'll try what speaking big will do—

[Advancing to him.

Why, yes, Captain Terrible; do you suppose I am to be daunted by your blustering? Bless me! if a long stride, a fierce brow, and a loud voice, were mortal, which of us should live to twenty? I'd have you to know, damn me—

FERDINAND
Draw your sword, draw your sword, thou amphibious thing! If you have the spirit of a man, let me see how you will prove it—

[Draws.

DONNA CLARA
Oh, Lord! what will become of me! hold, hold, for heaven's sake! what, will nothing but fighting satisfy you?—I'll do any thing in reason—don't be so hasty.

FERDINAND
Oh, thou egregious dastard! you won't fight, then?

DONNA CLARA
No, by no means. I'll settle this matter in another way.—
[Aside]
What will become of me?

FERDINAND
Thy hand shakes so, thou wilt not be able to sign a paper, though it were ready for thee; therefore, observe what I say to you.

DONNA CLARA
Yes, sir.

FERDINAND
And if thou darest to disobey, or murmur at the smallest article—

DONNA CLARA
Yes, sir.

FERDINAND
First then, own thou art a coward.

DONNA CLARA
Yes, sir.

FERDINAND
Unworthy of Leonora.

DONNA CLARA
Yes, sir.

FERDINAND
Return instantly to Salamanca.

DONNA CLARA [Seeing **LEONORA**]
Ha, Leonora! not till I have chastised you for your insolence.

[Draws.

[Enter **LEONORA**, and runs between them.

LEONORA
Heavens! what do I see! fighting! for shame, Ferdinand! draw your sword on a—stranger!

[She holds **FERDINAND**.

FERDINAND
Don't hold me.

DONNA CLARA
Hold him fast, madam—you can't do him a greater kindness.

FERDINAND [Struggling]
Dear Leonora!

DONNA CLARA
Thou miserable coward! thou egregious dastard! thou poltroon! by what name shall I call thee?

FERDINAND
Do you hear him, Leonora?

DONNA CLARA
Hold him fast, madam—I am quite in a fever with my rage at him. Madam, that fellow never should pretend to you: he was just ready to sign a paper I had prepared for him, renouncing all right and title to you.

FERDINAND [To **LEONORA**]
By heaven you injure, me!

DONNA CLARA
He had just consented to leave this city, and was actually upon his knees to me for mercy.

FERDINAND
Can I bear this?

LEONORA
Patience, dear Ferdinand.

DONNA CLARA
When seeing you coming, he plucked up a little spirit, because he knew you would prevent us, and drawing out his unwilling sword, which hung dangling like a dead weight by his side there, he began to flourish it about just as I do now, madam.

FERDINAND
Nothing shall restrain me—loose me, or by my wrongs, I shall think you are confederate with him. Now, madam, I see why you were so anxious to prevent me from chastising that coxcomb. It was not your love of me, but your fears for him—ungrateful woman!

LEONORA
Dear Ferdinand, rely upon it you are mistaken—don't trust appearances.

FERDINAND
Incomparable sex! we are their fools so often, they think nothing too gross to pass upon us—'sdeath! weathercocks, wind, and feathers, are nothing. Woman, woman, is the true type of mutability—and to be false to me for such a thing as that—I could cut such a man out of a sugared cake—I believe a confectioner made him.

LEONORA
Have you done yet?

FERDINAND
No, nor ever shall till you satisfy me. Then adieu—you shall see me no more, but you shall hear of me. I'll find your Narcissus, that precious flower-pot. I'll make him an example. All the wrongs I have suffered from you shall be revenged on him. My name shall be as terrible to all future coxcombs, as broad day-light to a decayed beauty, or a wet Sunday to a powdered citizen.

[Exeunt.

SCENE II.—Changes to the Hotel

Two Doors are placed obliquely, at opposite Sides of the Stage, as entrances to different Chambers.
Table and Chairs.

Enter **LAZARILLO**.

LAZARILLO
I have often heard that gentlemen, that is fine gentlemen, had no conscience; but I believe the truth is,
they have no stomachs: they seem to think of every thing but eating, and, for my part, I think of nothing
else. But here comes one of my masters.

[Enter **DONNA CLARA**, with a Paper.

DONNA CLARA
Has Don Pedro been here to enquire for me?

LAZARILLO
Truly, sir, I can't tell.

DONNA CLARA
Was he here?

LAZARILLO
Ay, that he was certainly.

DONNA CLARA
Did he leave nothing with you for me?

LAZARILLO
Not that I know of.

DONNA CLARA
What, no money?

LAZARILLO
Money!

DONNA CLARA
Ay, money. I expected a purse with two hundred pistoles.

LAZARILLO
I believe I have made a small mistake. The purse belongs to this master, and I gave it to the other.
[Aside]

Are you certain you expected a purse with two hundred pistoles?

DONNA CLARA
Certain—yes—what does the fellow stare at?

LAZARILLO
You are sure they were not for another gentleman that shall be nameless?

DONNA CLARA
Is the booby drunk?

LAZARILLO
It must be with wind then. Why, sir, I did receive a purse with the sum you mention, and from Don Pedro, but whether it was intended for you is a point that requires some consideration.

DONNA CLARA
What did Don Pedro say to you?

LAZARILLO
I'll tell you, sir. Friend, says Don Pedro, there are two hundred pistoles for your master.

DONNA CLARA
Well, dolt-head! and who is your master?

LAZARILLO
There's the point now—there's the puzzle. Ah, sir, there are many things you would not find it easy to explain, though you was educated at Salamanca, and are no doubt a great scholar.

DONNA CLARA
Give me the money, fool; and no more of your impertinence.

LAZARILLO
There it is, sir. Heaven do you good with it: I think I know some people who would be glad of just that sum, especially if they thought they had a right to it.

DONNA CLARA
No more—I expect Don Pedro. Bid Borachio get a good dinner; and here, take this letter of credit, lock it up carefully, I shall have occasion for a good deal of cash, and this way 'tis most portable: be careful of it, and make no mistakes; I expect dinner to be ready as soon as I return.

[Exit.

[**LAZARILLO**, alone.

You shall not wait a moment. This is the pleasantest order I have yet received from either of my masters. Here comes Borachio—I'll try if my host understands any thing of a table.

[Enter **BORACHIO**.

Signior Borachio, or Master Borachio, or Don Joseph de Borachio, you come most opportunely. We must have a dinner immediately.

BORACHIO
Name your hour. I am always prepared; two hours hence, an hour, half an hour;—my cooks are the readiest fellows—

LAZARILLO
Ay, but this must not be one of your every-day dinners, the first thing comes to hand, tossed up and warmed over again, neither hot nor cold, like a day in the beginning of April—that's villainous.

BORACHIO
Do you think I have kept the first tavern in the city so long, not to know how to please a gentleman?

LAZARILLO
Some gentlemen are easily pleased; other gentlemen are hard to be pleased; now I'm of the latter order.

BORACHIO
Gentleman, forsooth!

LAZARILLO
A gentleman's gentleman: that is, my master's master in most things, but in the business of his eating, absolute and uncontrolable: but come, Master Borachio, let us have your idea of a dinner.

BORACHIO
Two courses, to be sure.

LAZARILLO
Two courses and a dessert.

BORACHIO
Five in the first, and seven in the second.

LAZARILLO
Good.

BORACHIO
Why, in the middle I would have a rich savoury soup.

LAZARILLO
Made with craw-fish—good!

BORACHIO
At the top, two delicate white trout, just fresh from the river.

LAZARILLO

Good! excellent! go on, go on.

BORACHIO
At the bottom, a roast duck.

LAZARILLO
A duck! a scavenger! an unclean bird! a waddling glutton; his bill is a shovel, and his body but a dirt cart: away with your duck—let me have a roast turkey, plump and full-breasted, his craw full with marrow.

BORACHIO
You shall have it.

LAZARILLO
Now for the side dishes.

BORACHIO
At one side stewed venison, at the other an English plum-pudding.

LAZARILLO
An English plum-pudding! that's a dish I am a stranger to. Now, Signior Borachio, to your second course.

BORACHIO
Roast lamb at the top, partridge at the bottom, jelly and omlette on one side, pig and ham at the other, and Olla Podrida in the middle.

LAZARILLO
All wrong, all wrong,—what should be at the top you put at the bottom, and two dishes of pork at the same side. It won't do—it will never do, I tell you.

BORACHIO
How would you have it? I can order it no better.

LAZARILLO
It will never do. Mind, I don't find fault with the things; the things are good enough, very good, but half the merit of a service consists in the manner in which you put it on the table. Pig and ham at the same side! why you might as well put a Hebrew Jew into the same stall at church with the Grand Inquisitor. Mind me, do but mind me; see now, suppose this floor was the table.
[Goes upon one Knee, and tears the Paper left him by his Master]
Here's the top, and there's the bottom—put your partridge here,—
[Places a piece of the Paper]
—your lamb there,—
[Another piece of the Paper]
—there's top and bottom—Your jelly in the middle,—
[Another piece of the Paper]
Olla Podrida and pig at this side together,—
[Two pieces of the Paper]
—and the omlette and ham at this—
[Two pieces more of the Paper]

There's a table laid out for you as it should be—

[Looking at it with great satisfaction.

[Enter **DONNA CLARA** and **DON PEDRO**.

DONNA CLARA
Hey-day! what are you about on your knees there?

LAZARILLO
Shewing mine host how to lay out your honour's dinner: I'm no novice at these matters—I'll venture a wager—there are the dishes.

DONNA CLARA
Get up, puppy—what's this? as I live, the letter of credit I left with him to put up for me, all torn to pieces!

LAZARILLO
Oh the devil! I was so full of the dinner, every thing else slipped out of my memory.
[Aside]
Upon my soul, sir, I quite forgot it. I was so taken up about the main chance, I quite forgot the value of the paper.

DONNA CLARA
Dolt! idiot! a letter of credit for no less than four hundred pistoles—what amends can you make for such unconceivable stupidity?

BORACHIO [To **LAZARILLO**]
The merit of a dinner consists, you know, in the manner in which you put the things on the table. This is a confounded dear dinner, truly.

LAZARILLO
Plague upon it, it was your fault, and not mine; it never would have happened if you had served up the course properly—pig and ham at the same side! Such a blunder was never heard of.

[Exit **BORACHIO**.

DONNA CLARA [To **DON PEDRO**]
What can I do with this fellow?

DON PEDRO
The mischief is not without remedy. You must take up the pieces, join them, and paste them on a sheet of paper. Your bankers won't refuse it.

DONNA CLARA
Hear you—do you understand Don Pedro?

LAZARILLO

Perfectly. But in truth, sir, Borachio's stupidity was enough to drive every thing out of one's memory. He wanted, sir—

DONNA CLARA
Silence! take these fragments, and join them as Don Pedro directed you. Make haste, and attend at dinner.

LAZARILLO
Yes, sir. They'll make twenty mistakes if I am not present to direct them.

[Exit.

DON PEDRO
Really, young gentleman, nothing could be more à-propos than your arrival. A day's delay longer had lost you your mistress, and a good portion into the bargain. Have you seen any thing of Ferdinand, your rival, since?

DONNA CLARA
Yes, and was upon the point of a most desperate combat; but your daughter stepped in, and he ran to her for protection: but I frightened him soundly.

DON PEDRO
Indeed!

[Enter **BORACHIO**.

BORACHIO
Gentlemen, your dinner will be ready in less than half an hour.

DON PEDRO
Half an hour! can't you get it sooner? to say the truth, I'm a little hungry.

BORACHIO
What was ordered for you can't be ready sooner.

DONNA CLARA
Let us have any thing that's ready. Appetite's the best sauce. What say you, Don Pedro?

DON PEDRO
Ay, ay—better than all the cooks in France.

[Exeunt.

[Enter **LAZARILLO** with a Napkin under his Arm.

LAZARILLO
Here, waiters! waiters! what, are the fellows deaf? I knew nothing would be done till I got among them.

[Enter **FIRST WAITER**, with a Dish.

FIRST WAITER
Who calls? here—

LAZARILLO
What have you got there? where are you going?

FIRST WAITER
To carry it to your master.

LAZARILLO
What is it?

FIRST WAITER
I don't know, the cook made it, not I.

LAZARILLO
Put it down, I'll carry it myself.

[Exit **FIRST WAITER**.

It smells well—what is it? I'll try.

[Takes a spoon out of his Pocket.

Like a good soldier, or good surgeon, I never go without my arms and my instruments.

[Tastes the Dish.

Excellent, faith—I'll try it again—better and better—but here it goes for master.

[**OCTAVIO** meets him as he is carrying in the Dish.

LAZARILLO
Cursed ill luck, here's my other master.

OCTAVIO
Where are you going?

LAZARILLO
Going, sir—sir, I was going—I was going to carry this in for your honour's dinner.

OCTAVIO
Carry in my dinner, before you knew I was come home!

LAZARILLO

Lord! sir, I knew you was coming home. I happened just now to pop my head out of the window, and saw you walking down the street, so I thought you would like to have your dinner on the table the moment you came in.

OCTAVIO
What have you got there?

LAZARILLO
'Tis a kind of a fricasee, very good, I promise you.

OCTAVIO
Let me have soup—what, do you bring meat before soup, you blockhead!

LAZARILLO
Lord, sir, nothing so common. In some parts of the world soup is the very last thing brought to the table.

OCTAVIO
That's not my custom—carry that back, and order some soup immediately.

LAZARILLO
Yes, sir.

OCTAVIO
How unfortunate! to have searched so much, and to have heard nothing of Donna Clara.

[Exit.

[**LAZARILLO**, pretending to go down, returns.

Now I may carry this to my first master.

[Goes into Donna Clara's Chamber.

[Enter **SECOND WAITER** with a Dish.

SECOND WAITER Where is this man? Lazarillo!

LAZARILLO [Running out]
Who calls? here I am.

SECOND WAITER Carry this to your master.

[Exit **SECOND WAITER**.

LAZARILLO
That I will—give it to me. I'll carry it to the first.

[Going towards Clara's Chamber, is called to Octavio's.

What do you want? here I am.

[Enter **FIRST WAITER** with a Dish.

FIRST WAITER
Here's a dish for your master.

LAZARILLO
You're an honest fellow. Come, stir, stir, get the soup as fast as possible.

[Exit **FIRST WAITER**.

If I can have the good fortune to serve them both without being discovered—

[Going towards Clara's Chamber, is called from Octavio's.

OCTAVIO [Within]
Lazarillo!

LAZARILLO
Coming! Coming!

[Enter **SECOND WAITER** with a Dish.

SECOND WAITER Where is this strange fellow, Lazarillo?

LAZARILLO
Who calls? here I am.

SECOND WAITER Do you attend one table, and we'll take care of the other.

LAZARILLO
Not at all, not at all, I'll take care of them both.

[Exit **SECOND WAITER**.

DONNA CLARA [From within]
Lazarillo!

LAZARILLO
Here.

OCTAVIO [Within]
Lazarillo!

LAZARILLO
Patience, a little patience. Coming!

[Enter **FIRST WAITER** with a Dish.

FIRST WAITER
Master—what's your name, here's a pudding.

LAZARILLO
A pudding! What pudding?

FIRST WAITER
An English plum-pudding.

LAZARILLO
Lay it down, lay it down.

[Exit **FIRST WAITER**.

This is a stranger, I must be civil to him. He looks like a Mulatto in the small-pox. Let's try how he tastes.

[Takes out his Spoon.

Excellent! Admirable! rich as marrow, and strong as brandy.

[Eats again.

This is meat and drink, no trusting outsides. This leopard-like pudding is most divine, I can't part with it.

[Eats again, and sits down.

[Enter **DONNA CLARA** with a Cane.

DONNA CLARA
I must get another servant. This fellow minds nothing. Where are you, rascal?
[Sees him]
There he is cramming himself instead of attending me.

OCTAVIO [Within]
Lazarillo!

LAZARILLO [Speaking with his mouth full]
In a moment, in a moment.

DONNA CLARA
What are you about there? don't you see me?

LAZARILLO
I was just—tasting this pudding for you—I promise you, sir—you'll like it.

DONNA CLARA
Why, 'tis all gone.

LAZARILLO
It slips down so fast, sir, you can't tell the taste of it till you eat a good deal.

DONNA CLARA [Beats him]
Taste that, and that, and that—

LAZARILLO
Hold, hold, sir, for heaven's sake! take care, sir! you have no right to more than one half of me, t'other belongs to another gentleman—oh! oh! oh!

[Enter **OCTAVIO**.

OCTAVIO
What's this! beating my servant! Loose your hold, sir! what right have you to strike my servant? a blow to the fellow who receives my wages, is an affront to me. You must account with me for this.

DONNA CLARA [Seeing **OCTAVIO**]
By all my hopes, Octavio!

LAZARILLO [Aside]
If this comes to a duel, and one of them falls, I am for the survivor.

OCTAVIO
You look surprised, sir! what, is this doctrine new to you?

DONNA CLARA
I am not much accustomed to menaces from those lips; do you not know me, Octavio?

OCTAVIO
Know you!

DONNA CLARA
Is my voice a stranger to you? must you have stronger proofs that I am Clara—if so, let this convince you.

OCTAVIO
O unexpected happiness! Art thou, indeed, my Clara? the same sincere, faithful, generous Clara, I knew and loved at Salamanca?

DONNA CLARA
The same, the very same. Don Pedro's in the next room; I'll step and explain what has happened, and send immediately for Leonora and Ferdinand.

[Exit.

LAZARILLO
May I take the liberty of offering my poor congratulations on this joyful occasion? Will you believe it, sir, I had a sort of an inkling, a divining, that something of this kind would happen; for I dreamt all last night of cats and dogs and a spread eagle.

OCTAVIO
Your dreams, I hope, go by contraries; and you shall be a witness of our harmony, for I intend to keep you in my service.

[Enter **DONNA CLARA**, **DON PEDRO**, **LEONORA**, **DON SANCHO**, and **FERDINAND**.

DON PEDRO
Joy, joy, I give you joy, this discovery has saved us all a great deal of perplexity. Our only strife now shall be, who will fill the greatest quantity of bumpers to the felicity of this double gemini of turtles.

DON SANCHO
Brother-in-law that is to be, give me your hand: we will presently drown all animosities in a bottle of honest Borachio's Burgundy.

[**LAZARILLO** steps forward.

LAZARILLO
To serve two masters long I strove in vain, Hard words or blows were all my toils could gain: But their displeasure now no more can move, If you—
[To the **AUDIENCE**]
—my kinder masters, but approve.

[Exeunt.

www.ingramcontent.com/pod-product-compliance
Lightning Source LLC
Chambersburg PA
CBHW021946040426
42448CB00008B/1259